Meet Tommy the Turtle in the latest book from
The Tales of Gripper the Crab

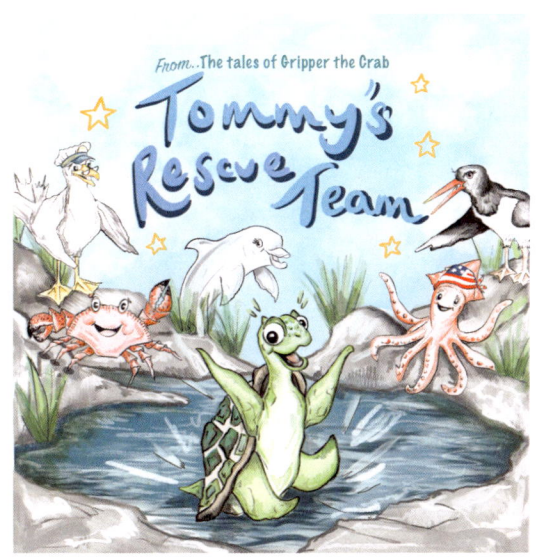

Written by Peter Butler

Illustrated by Kathryn Pow

Copyright © 2024 Peter Butler

Published by Peter Butler Books

The right of Peter Butler to be identified of the author of this work has been asserted by him in accordance with the Copyright, Designs and Patents Act 1988.

The right of Kathryn Pow to be identified of the illustrator of this work has been asserted by her in accordance with the Copyright, Designs and Patents Act 1988.

All rights reserved. No part of this book may be reproduced, transmitted or stored in an information retrieval system by any means, without prior permission from the publisher.

A CIP catalogue record of this book is available from the British Library.

ISBN 978-1-7392993-1-6

Hiya, it's me again, Barnacle Boppy.

For those who haven't heard of me yet, I live in a fisherman's hut at Porthmeric in Cornwall. Why? Because it's beautiful here; bright blue sea, lovely golden sands, and a rock pool where lots of wonderful sea creatures live.

I have become best friends with them and they tell me about their amazing adventures. You see, they have promised to look after one another as all good families must. That means when one of them is in trouble the rest gather together and help them.

Because I love their heart warming exploits so much I have written them into six stories for you all to enjoy with me. The book series is called

'The Tales of Gripper the Crab'.

I know lots of you have already read the first one called 'Heidi's New Home', and I thank you for the many kind comments.

This is the second book. It's titled 'Tommy's Rescue Team' and is a reminder to us all about the shameful increase of pollution in our seas. There is a very important request from Tommy at the end.

Love you all

Barnacle Boppy

Meet the Cast!

You might know some of Gripper's friends from the first book, Heidi's New Home, but today you'll meet some new characters!

They'll all be popping up in each of the stories in the Gripper the Crab series!

I'm Tommy the Turtle and I'm daft as a brush,
I talk too quickly 'cos I'm always in a rush!

My name's Gripper and I'm a crab,
I live in a rock pool - it's really fab!

I'm Gulliver the Seagull and I'm a wise old bird,
I keep the beach safe, as you might have heard.

I'm Dotty Dolphin, and I live in the Bay.
The Rock Pool crew are my best friends,
they make me smile every day.

I'm Olah the Oyster Catcher, but they are not
what I eat. The Sandhopper's here jump up and
down, so they're my favourite treat

"Oh, blistering barnacles!" He cries.

"Here I am in the sea

Hungry as a turtle can be.

Where are the shrimps and whelks for me?"

Dotty Dolphin hears him and swims over.

"Tommy," she says. "You missed the Rockpool breakfast rush! Didn't your friends leave you anything to eat?"

"Not even the tiniest nibble," Tommy sighs.

"Well," says Dotty. "Four eyes are better than two. Let me help you."

Dotty dives beneath the waves. In no time at all she pops up a few metres away and calls...

"Tommy! Tommy! Have no fear!

I've found your breakfast over here...

A juicy jellyfish, fresh and yummy -

This will fill your empty tummy!"

Hungrier than ever, Tommy paddles quickly to the jellyfish and gobbles it up.

It looks like jellyfish...

It smells like jellyfish...

But it doesn't taste like jellyfish.

He turns to Dotty with a worried look on his face.

"Are you alright, Tommy?" Dotty asks.

"Dotty, I can't swallow this jellyfish!"

"Oh dear," says Dotty. "Let me look. Open wide!"

She peers into Tommy's mouth. The jellyfish is stuck just behind his tiny turtle tonsils.

"We need something long and thin to get the jellyfish out, Tommy. My big dolphin nose won't fit," says Dotty.

The beach is nearby. She scans the sand and sees Olah the Oyster Catcher.

"That's it! Olah can help. She has a beak that's perfect for the job!"

Tommy follows Dotty to the beach, coughing and spluttering thanks to the jellyfish stuck in his throat. They reach the shore just as Olah is finishing her breakfast.

"Hello, Tommy," says the dainty bird. "How's my favourite turtle this sunny morning?"

"Not... very... well," Tommy croaks. "Just... ate... jellyfish... Stuck...in... throat!"

"Oh no, you poor thing! Let me take it out for you. Open wide!"

Olah tries and tries to hook the jellyfish with her beak. But it just won't move. There's only one thing for it: it's time to call on Captain Gulliver the Seagull!

The animals call out together, "Gulliver! Gulliver! We need your help!"

Captain Gulliver swoops across and lands at Olah's side.

"Now then, now then, whatever is the matter?" he asks.

Olah explains the situation while Tommy looks sadder and sadder.

Gulliver peers into Tommy's mouth, he gasps angrily.

"That's not a jellyfish!" he cries. "It's a horrid plastic bag - and there are baby fish trapped in it!

Millions of fish and turtles are lost every year because of plastic bags that smell and look like jellyfish. Humans throw them away without thinking about where they might end up.

Bought bags and free bags, should not be in the sea bags!" Gulliver stamps his foot.

"OK, everybody, action stations! There's no time to lose. We must save our Tommy and the baby fish."

Having heard all the commotion, along scuttles Gripper the Crab to find everyone looking very worried indeed.

Once the friends have explained the situation to Gripper, he is determined to help. "What shall I do?" He asks Gulliver.

"Find help Gripper. Quickly. Olah and I will stay here and look after Tommy."

"Aye, aye, Captain!" Gripper says, before diving down to the sea bed.

Underneath the waves, Gripper desperately searches for someone - or something - that can free the plastic bag from Tommy's throat. Suddenly, he hears singing.

Scuttling in the direction of the voice, he sees a funny looking creature sitting on a rock. It is singing to itself, and it does not sound like it comes from Porthmeric.

♪ "I'm Billie the Squid

Don't know how I did

But I've come a very long way.

One heck of a trip

Without a slip

To here from the USA." ♪

Gripper calls across to him, "I'm so sorry to interrupt your song, but I need your help!"

Billy pushes himself off his rock and swims over. "Hey, man. What's up?"

Gripper explains the problem.

"I'm your man, Crabby! Look, I have 8 arms and 2 long tentacles, and they're darn powerful. Where is this guy?"

Gripper leads Billy over to Tommy, Olah and Gulliver on the shore. "Help has arrived!" He calls.

Billy reaches a tentacle out to Tommy and shakes his flipper. "You must be Tommy. I'm Billy the Squid from the USA, and I've come to save you."

Tommy opens his mouth wide so that Billy can peer inside.

"Piece of cake. That plastic bag is no match for my powerful tentacles!"

He turns to the others. "Y'all go and sit on that rock. I'll wrap my tentacles around the top of the bag and get tugging."

Minutes pass, but there's no sign of the bag.

Gripper can't bear to wait any longer. Scuttling over to Billy, he asks nervously,

"Any luck Billy?"

Billy stops tugging. "This darn bag won't budge, man. It's totally stuck!"

Tommy looks terrified, so Gripper heads back to the rock where the others are anxiously waiting.

"It's no use. Billy the Squid can't get the plastic bag out. We need a plan B."

The friends look at each other, but nobody has a clue what to do.

Then, suddenly, Gripper makes everyone jump!

"AHA! I've got an idea! While Billy is tugging, I'll tickle Tommy under his chin. It might make him sneeze or cough and the bag will come flying out!"

"What a good idea, Gripper." says Olah. "We could all sing!"

♪ "Round and round the rock pool,
Gripper took a spin.
One step, two steps,
and a tickly under chin!" ♪

"Gulliver, maybe you could lend him a feather?
That would make it even more ticklier!"

Billy is not amused or as easy to convince. "WHAT?" he mocks.

"What birdbrain came up with that load of scallops? It'll never work!"

"Hey! Less of the 'birdbrain', Squid!" says Gulliver crossly.

"But it has to be worth a try, Billy!" says Gripper. "What have we got to lose?"

Billy seems to be considering it, and Gripper isn't about to give up.

"Look, I've heard Tommy sneeze loads of times. He's very good at it. I just know this will work!"

"OK Kid, if it means you'll let me get on with saving your turtle friend, I'll try your dumb idea. But I'm telling you, it won't work."

Billy attaches a tentacle to the plastic bag in Tommy's throat and the countdown begins.

"THREE...TWO ... ONE...PULL!"

Billy heaves with all his might, and Gripper gently puts the feather under Tommy's chin and starts tickling...

But after a lot of tugging and tickling, there isn't a sign of the tiniest cough or sneeze. Billy stops pulling and shakes his head. "I told you it wouldn't work."

Gripper stops tickling and turns away. He starts to crawl sadly towards his friends, but Olah calls out, "Wait, Gripper! Turn around! Look!"

Gripper turns around and stares, his mouth dropping open wider and wider.

Tommy Turtle is raising his head. He takes the biggest breath you ever did see, then lets out the mightiest sneeze you ever did hear!

"AH....CHOOOOO!!!"

The sneeze and the shock knocks everyone off their feet.

The plastic bag full of baby fish comes shooting out of Tommy's mouth, with Billy's tentacle still wrapped around the handles!

It flies through the air and into the sea where it bursts. All the baby fish swim out of the bag and into the rolling waves, clapping their fins and singing in excitement.

♪ "Tommy the turtle got into a pickle

But all it took was a tug and a tickle

To save him from plastic polluting our seas

With the biggest, loudest, sneeziest sneeze!" ♪

"AH....CHOOOOO!!!"

"Well, that seems to have done the trick!" smiles a very relieved Gripper.

"It sure has!" says Billy, picking himself up and rubbing his tentacle.

Olah is first to Tommy's side and gives him a great big cuddle.

"Tommy, my little friend, you're safe! We were all so worried - are you alright?"

Tommy looks dazed, but smiles. "I only went out for a breakfast snack. At one point there, I didn't think I was coming back!"

"Yes, but you were saved by Gripper and our new friend Billy. Oh, Tommy, we're so happy because we all love you so much."

Gulliver joins in with the cheers and claps his wings together.

"Well done, team. Tommy and the baby fish are all safe."

Tommy speaks "I want to thank my rock pool family - old and new - for saving my life. I was lucky others are not. Now we must make sure this doesn't happen to any other turtle or crab or even shark or eel. All sea creatures should be safe from plastic pollution!

So, I would like to ask every boy or girl reading this book to make me a very special promise....

...please, always collect plastic bags and other rubbish and take it with with you when you leave the beach. If we don't dispose of our rubbish safely, one day there will more plastic in the sea than fish, and that would be terrible, wouldn't it? Please help keep us all safe."

Gulliver claps his wings again."Hear! Hear!"

This is a special day, so let's end it on a happy note and sing the little fishes song one more time'

🎵 "Tommy the turtle got into a pickle

But all it took was a tug and a tickle

To save him from plastic polluting our seas

With the biggest, loudest, sneeziest sneeze!" 🎵

"AH....CHOOOOO!!!"

***

HURRAH! Another happy ending and that's it from me, Barnacle Boppy, in Porthmeric.

Don't forget what Tommy said, will you?

I know you won't.

Night night.

Did you know there's another book to enjoy?

Heidi's New Home is available now.

Why not collect them all?

To learn more about our books
pop over to our website

www.gripperthecrab.com

We'd love to see you there!

Want to get in touch?
Email us at info@gripperthecrab.com

You could even share your own stories and pictures!

www.gripperthecrab.com

www.ingramcontent.com/pod-product-compliance
Lightning Source LLC
Chambersburg PA
CBRC091452160426
43209CB00023B/1876